I Won't Be!

I WON'T BE!

A DECLARATION OF YOU

By: Laurie Daniels

XULON PRESS

Xulon Press
2301 Lucien Way #415
Maitland, FL 32751
407.339.4217
www.xulonpress.com

© 2022 by Laurie Daniels

All rights reserved solely by the author. The author guarantees all contents are original and do not infringe upon the legal rights of any other person or work. No part of this book may be reproduced in any form without the permission of the author.

Due to the changing nature of the Internet, if there are any web addresses, links, or URLs included in this manuscript, these may have been altered and may no longer be accessible. The views and opinions shared in this book belong solely to the author and do not necessarily reflect those of the publisher. The publisher therefore disclaims responsibility for the views or opinions expressed within the work.

Unless otherwise indicated, Scripture quotations taken from the King James Version (KJV) – *public domain.*

Unless otherwise indicated, Scripture quotations taken from the Holy Bible, New International Version (NIV). Copyright © 1973, 1978, 1984, 2011 by Biblica, Inc.™. Used by permission. All rights reserved.

Paperback ISBN-13: 978-1-6628-4414-0

Dedication Page

This book is dedicated to my family who has always been my inspiration. They are the reason I was able to persevere in writing this book.

I want to thank all of those who will read this book. Thank you for trusting me with these words. I thank you for changing where you see necessary and most importantly, thank you for not giving up on your dreams.

I give all the praise to my Lord and Savior Jesus Christ. To Him be the Glory! Amen.

Table of Contents

Title...i
Copyrights..ix
Dedication.. vii
Quote xiii
Conversation..1
I Won't Be! (The Poem) 7
Declaration of You 9

DECLARATION I (Who Says?) 15

   1. Tête-à-tête........................ 17
      a. Resistance is Futile! 20
      b. Identity Theft 24
      c. To Be Seen........................ 29
      d. Communication....................31

DECLARATION II (Walk it Out) 33

   1. Tête-à-tête........................ 35
      a. Walk (Peripateo) 37
      b. Your Walk is Uniquely You........... 40

DECLARATION III (Bust A Move) 43

1. Tête-à-tête.......................... 45
   a. The Rut Stops Here 46
   b. Procrastination.................... 47
   c. Appetizer or Main Dish 49

DECLARATION IV (Run this Race)..............53

1. Tête-à-tête.......................... 55
   a. Run this Race!..................... 56
   b. Your Place in Life................. 58
   c. Hold Your Peace.................... 60
2. Tête-à-tête.......................... 62
   a. Mountain Mover 64

DECLARATION V (Perseverance) 67

1. Tête-à-tête.......................... 68
   a. It's a Fight worth Fighting............ 70
   b. Be Empowered with the Right Motive 72

DECLARATION VI (Grit) 75

1. Tête-à-tête.......................... 77
   a. True Grit 79
   c. Arise!..............................81

DECLARATION VII (Humility) 87

1. Tête-à-tête.......................... 89
   a. Your Greatest Battle..................91

DECLARATION VIII (The Beauty of You) 95

    1. Tête-à-tête........................... 97
        a. The Philosophies of Past Hero's 100
        b. Richly Scented 103

Tête-à-tête 106

Final Exultation 108

Declaration of You Questionnaire 110

Thank You!..................................... 111

Quote

"Don't let anyone build your world for you. Because they will always build it too small."

Dallas Daniels Sr.

Conversation

WHILE I WAS WRITING THIS BOOK, OUR COUNTRY was going through a pandemic, and we were all wearing masks. I prayed that by the time this book is published we would be out of it. Still, interestingly, as these masks became more fashionable with each passing week, they were noticeably created in all shapes and sizes with unique designs and colors. Some had words, some had pictures, and others had signs and symbols. People seemed to be accepting this fashion as the new norm. However, I resisted that notion because I didn't want to live my life permanently behind something that was temporal. Yet, there are less visible masks we sometimes wear strictly to protect ourselves. These masks allow us to pretend to be something we aren't or someone else altogether. We may even sometimes wear them out of fear, rejection, hurt, or insecurity. When we continue to hide behind masks, we close ourselves off from the real us allowing ourselves to be intimidated by the world around us, but we can break free from these masks if we take a stand.

I Won't Be!

This book could be the first defense against falsifying our identity. "*I Won't Be!*" is a bold declaration of not allowing your world to be built for you. I admit, it will take more than just saying, "I won't be!" You will have to act upon your confession to minimize the masks which facilitate the reason you wear them. "I won't be" means fighting against the things that would hold you back from being you. "I won't be" will dare you to refuse your face to be trapped behind a looking glass.

We want to be a part of something that makes us feel important. It's human nature to vie for attention and approval especially from those we respect and with whom we are closest, but at what expense? Will you recognize who you are? So, to be in the reindeer game we hide the thing that makes us, us. We use this alter ego to transform into whatever culture dictates at that moment. It could affect our work, our family, just hanging out with friends, even our church, nonetheless, we often use a façade to fit in.

Under these masks, we carry insecurities that feed the fears that stop us from being ourselves. Instead of respecting who we are as a person, we become transformed into people-pleasers, doing whatever it takes to be whatever the relationship demands. When will we decide what kind of world we want to build? When will we decide to be okay with our best, yet imperfect self and embrace it? Sometimes we look at our imperfections as faults instead of that which makes us unique.

Throughout this book, I will continue to challenge you to declare, "I won't be!" It will take guts to stand and fight for your identity. I hope that I provoke you to be the architect of your life. Anything less just won't do!

Let, *"I Won't Be!"* provoke you to construct your world even in the face of opposition. May this declaration challenge you to come out of abusive relationships, negative influences of social media, and even self-mutilation. This book may even be used to help you be truly honest with yourself. What are you saying to yourself? Do you have low self-esteem? Do you feel you're not good enough, smart enough, dark, or light enough? Can you embrace who you are at this moment? Let's take this journey together as you transform into the best version of yourself.

My best version is still developing as I grow in my relationship with Jesus Christ. He helps me to see myself as He sees me. I recall the fear of going back to work after being a stay-at-home mom. We raised four children and I enjoyed every moment of being home with them. However, when they reached school age, I remember the Lord showing me that He wanted me to get back into the work force. First, we needed the money and secondly, it was time for me to go into the next season of my life. My husband had been providing for us solely for all those years, so it was now time for me to help financially.

I was used to being in an atmosphere I could control therefore, stepping out into the work world actually frightened me. Although the Lord had shown He was with me every step of the way, I still snuggled with the mask of intimidation. My first job was a bus monitor for a summer camp program. I attended to about twenty kids ranging from ages five to fourteen years old. I rode around with the bus driver as he picked up each child to take them to camp and to make matters worse, my second oldest son was one of the kids on that bus. I couldn't allow him to see my fear under that mask. I also couldn't allow him to see me as weak. That's not the mom he knew! Still, I wondered, could I command the authority I had at home with someone else's children? Would they respect me? Would they listen to me? Those kids challenged me every day.

Day after day, the Lord showed me I had the authority to command respect because He dwells inside me. Do you want to know the funniest thing about all this? I didn't have to command anything from them. All I had to do was just let them be kids and enforce the safety rules. Sure, there was always one kid that tried me, but I learned as I interacted with them, they all were rather good kids. I was laughing and joking with them by the end of the summer program. I learned authority is a posture that isn't necessarily rigid. I also learned something about myself that summer. It wasn't the job that intimidated me but the fear of appearing less than to my son. I had to face that fear and overcome it, and do you know what? I did.

My hope in authoring this book is to help others see the blessing they are to this world and discover the value of who they are and what they can be. When we value other's opinions more than our own, we become a bargain version of ourselves living in a world already too small.

I hope this declaration isn't just a poem that rhymes but words that empower your change. There is a scripture that helps me which says, [1] "By your patience possess your souls" (NKJV, 1982, Luke 21:19). In Blue letter Bible Greek word for soul is *psychē* means, "the mind, emotions, the seat of your feelings." It will take determination not to be the victim of masked faces because hiding only feeds your fears. If you continue to hide behind masks, you have already allowed society to define you.

I have read that sociologist and psychologist believe family, religion, society, and environment shape our thinking and ideas about life, and have both good and bad influences. Still, breaking away from bad influences take courage. My faith in Christ is my strength and my foundation. Would you agree that we all need help from time to time from someone stronger and mightier than we are in this life to help resist those alluring influences? If you are a person of faith, then you can ground your identity in that faith and discover who you are. You may find out that you're nothing like the world around you nor what it tries to tell you, you are. This book is an expansion of a positive and bold declaration.

When we realize that our declaration and words create our world, we can take control without feeling powerless. My husband has always told our children, "Never let anyone build your world for you, because they'll always build it too small." That is wise advice and worthy of consideration. We shouldn't want someone else's idea of what our lives should be like to overshadow our own. It's a good idea to get wise counsel to help you to think and evaluate yourself. Wise counsel should support your ideas and help you navigate through your decision process.

To aid you with your resistance, I've taken each stanza at a time to help make this your declaration or you can add your own. Each declaration is personal and the only one who can make that stand is you. I've also added Tête-à-tête to take a moment to gather your thoughts. You're not hopeless when you believe your life is worth the fight! It's time to raise the shield of resistance!

So, let's do this. I want you to buy yourself a couple of journals and a planner. Turn one of the journals into a vision journal. A vision journal is where you'll put pictures of your dreams and ideas. Write down what each picture represents. Next, use your planner to map out your day-to-day goals, both short term and long-term. Finally, use the remaining journal to keep track of your thoughts and feelings. They don't have to be expensive books, but this is the way to help you work toward bringing your dreams to fruition. Come on, let's do this!

"I Won't Be!" (The poem)

I Won't be
What other people speak, or say or see
Or hide behind a mask to be other than me

I won't be
Other people's plans, or dreams or talk
This life was given to me to walk

I won't be
Some side order waiting for a second chance
I will make my own music, dance my own dance

I won't be
stopped, quit, or lose my place
There's a prize for me
In this human race

It may seem darkest before the sunrise
Armed and dressed for the battle
I will rise

I Won't Be!

Standing up, I'm all about it
I'll fight my way through
times seem down
I won't give in
Anything less than that
won't do!

There may be tears and pain along the way
But I know who I am
On my knees, I will pray

I'm proud and beautiful been set free
Anything less than who I am
I Won't Be!

A Declaration of You

I believe many people have an inner struggle with being themselves. Some describe this as having an identity crisis. The psychologist Erickson describes it as, "failure to achieve ego (self-image) identity during adolescence" (Erickson, Stage 4 Identity vs Role Confusion 1902-1994, p. 85). This reasonably explains why we struggle from time to time with being ourselves around peers, coworkers, and friends. Our ego (self-image) lacks confidence in who we are (food for thought). We also watch movies, talk shows, and even reality shows that perpetuate this. I'm by no means saying we shouldn't enjoy entertainment, but we shouldn't be captivated by it in our own mind and body.

I like the reality show, "The Masked Singer." It's an American singing competition television series. Part of The Masked Singer franchise features celebrities singing songs while wearing head-to-toe costumes concealing their identities. During the series, each celebrity is unmasked one by one as the competition progresses.

I Won't Be!

When celebrities are unmasked, some tell the story of how they were ostracized in some way. They often testify they were shy or suffered public ridicule and wearing the mask allowed them to be themselves without judgement. Although the masks gave them boldness to be totally liberated, they still concealed their true identity while fighting underneath to be themselves.

It's interesting to be able to peek into the lives of celebrities who hid themselves behind the mask. In some ways, the competition helped them face insecurities that held them back. Beneath those masks they struggled with why they felt the need to wear them privately and publicly on the competition. When the mask was removed at the end of the show, the celebrities revealed their identities and chose not to allow others' opinions to shape them. Like contestants on The Masked Singer, we often put on elaborate performances on our stage of life to protect our identity. Yet life has a way of drawing back the curtain and revealing the true Wizard of Oz behind it.

Who's going to declare you? It's your responsibility to reveal your whole persona pronouncing your success, dreams and worth. You gird yourself with a positive posture that refuses to be hidden behind a mask by doing so. I'm reminded of the young timid girl I used to be that took four young children to the utility company. Although that may not sound too bad, being timid could have been crippling for me if I didn't learn to stand up for my children and protect them. As I sat with my daughter in a baby stroller waiting for my name to be called, my youngest son was beside me, but my older sons decided to make a game out of one crawling under the cubicle and the other one rolling on the floor.

As I tried to calm them down, two elderly women with their smug faces and daring stare began to whisper to each other. The first one whispered, "Look at that poor little girl with all those children," as she leaned into the other woman's ear. The second woman nodded as she sat pompously in her seat. "She can't even get them under control," squawked the second woman. On top of that, I weighed only about 100 lbs. I felt what shaped my identity was what older people thought of me. In my mind I thought, "Yup, here I am looking like this little girl with no father in sight to help me out."

I felt ashamed and embarrassed especially since my husband couldn't accompany me that day. I thought to myself, "How could I stand up for them when I couldn't stand up for myself?" I had a few choice words for those elderly women, but I was taught to respect my elders, so I kept my words to myself. When I got home from paying my bill, I called my mom and cried, "Mom!" I balled over the phone. "Don't ever look at a young girl with children and assume she is just some little girl playing house. "What happened?" she asked. I told my mom about the two elderly women at the utility company. My mom replied, "I'll remember what you told me." That was a battle I had to win first for me, then for them. How those women viewed me wasn't my true identity as I was immensely proud to be a wife and a mother despite their stares of disapproval. Recalling that situation made me think how this poem could motivate others to stand up for themselves.

Against whom or what do you need to take your stand? Maybe it's yourself. Do you desire to have a healthier lifestyle? Then you must stand against unhealthy eating habits. Even if things are progressing slowly, resist the urge to give up and learn through the process. Perhaps you've become addicted to drugs or a toxic relationship. Maybe negative words planted in your mind since you were a child still shape your ideas. I don't know what challenges you, but you do. Declare you won't allow those things to keep you down!

When I think of people who fought to hold onto their identity, I think of "*Roots*," an American television miniseries, based on Alex Haley's 1976 novel "*Roots*." I remember the intensity, deep emotional sadness, and anger, not just because Africans were taken from their home country, people, and culture, but due to the violence they suffered in the attempt to strip them of their identity. Some were stripped by breaking their will through beatings. Others were severely oppressed in their spirit being chained, raped, and torn from their families. It was truly a physical and mental struggle for them to maintain their identity while maintaining their dignity.

We wage war against people and things to maintain our own identity today. If we look back at history, we'll see all kinds of people who wrestled and then won the fights for themselves. There is always a torch to carry and pass on to the next generation. Understand, it's your fight and you must strategize how to wage wars both within and without.

Africans paid a great price to hold on to who they were and not allow themselves to be assimilated into another culture and lose their identity. I hope this book opens your eyes to recognize where your battle lies. I created some tools to help you resist those things that would attempt to consume you or strip you of your identity. Don't be afraid of challenges as there will always be something designed to hold you back from your goals and dreams. The only question left is, "Will you pick up your torch and run your race?"

DECLARATION I (Who Says?)

I won't be…

What other people speak, or say or see

Or hide behind a mask to be other than me

Tête-à-tête

Here you are, just you and your heart, having a conversation with yourself. This is where you begin to peel off your masks. This is where you make your declaration and say, "I won't be…"

There are many people who have been hurt by words spoken by others. Have you ever heard the saying, "Sticks and stones may break my bones, but names will never hurt me?" Well, negative names and words can hurt! They can go down into the inner most part of the soul. If allowed, those words can shape your world. The world that negative words create can affect the hearer's destiny. When those negative names or words aren't addressed, we put-up barriers to hide from those hurtful words. Thus, we pretend to be someone else to avoid dealing with the hurt they've caused. In a way, it's self-preservation. However, positive words can be just as effective and free you from hiding your true self. The question is, who determines what your world will be? *Captain Planet and the Planeteers* was an American animated, environmentalist superheroes of the 1990's.[2] As they fought to save the planet from pollutants, he would remind his young audience that they had the power to change and save their world. As he ended each episode, Captain Planet reminded them, "The power is yours!"

Who says? Most of the time we are built up or torn down by the people that are closest to us. Consider a child who was told they will never amount to anything. When they grow up, they've carried those words into adulthood. So, the negative words spoken to them can become a hindrance to their success in life. However, the child who has been encouraged to reach for the sky more likely grows up to become successful in all their endowers. The one "Who say" does make a difference. It depends on to whom you are listening and what is being said. Is what's being said building you up or tearing you down?

I like the song Lauren Daigle sings entitled, "You Say," and the verse I pinpoint is, "in You I find my worth, in You I find my identity." Too often, people walk around not knowing who they are because they don't realize their worth nor value. We therefore often look to those who make a positive impression on us. When I listen to what God says about me then I know my worth and discover my identity. His Word always reveals to me who I am to Him. I can then wage my war against any negative influence by listening to what God's Word says about me.

You, too, must wage war by declaring who you are. Be aware, the war isn't always fought outside of us but often from within. So, I'd like to know, how you feel about yourself? When you look deep within, who do you see? Do you like yourself? If not, why? The battle of identifying who you are starts with you. This battle is won or lost in the image of your mind. Who helped create that image? How you care for yourself will be a product of who you see inside. It's important to have a strong self-image however, it's created by the thoughts you cling to. The good news is, you don't have to yield to any bad images or negative influences if you choose not to. You decide what you accept or reject. No matter how long it's been, you have the power to change. You don't need to pretend or hide behind a false identity. Can I share with you one way to shed that right now? Forgive. Forgiveness is one of the strongest antidotes to healing.

Your self-esteem is particularly important. It can give you the strength to move forward if you believe in yourself. Although I mention self often, this is not necessarily a self-help book as we all need help from God or a higher power. We weren't meant to live this life on our own. We have also been given others to help us in this life. This book isn't about being selfish either but of possessing an awareness of your identity, talents, ability, and worth. I don't believe God created anyone to be worthless or useless. Still, how you view yourself whether debased or confident will affect how you decide to live your life. This choice may also help design the mask behind which you hide.

Resistance Is Futile!

My family and friends know that I am a Treky. I like all the Star Trek series and movies including William Shatner along with other space movies. Yet, Star Trek Voyager is my favorite series because I like Captain Janeway (Kate Mulgrew). I've seen her be courageous, vulnerable, and win and lose battles not just fighting with outside enemies but with inner mental and emotional ones too. There was even an episode when religion challenged her scientific beliefs.

My favorite episodes are when Captain Janeway encounters her nemesis known as the Borg. The Borg are mechanical enhanced beings who capture and assimilate other species by injecting Nanoprobes into the victim's body. Nanoprobes are a form of nanotechnology, and their primary function is to facilitate the assimilation of other species into the Collective Hive Mind. These mechanical cells also assimilate other species through their bloodstream via injection tubes thereby transforming the victim into the Borgs collective, to share one mind and mission, perfection!

As these fictitious nemeses strive for perfection, they have no qualm knowing, "resistance is futile!" I see the same scenario being played out in everyday life through television, social media, magazines, movies, peer pressure, and circumstances. The Borg isn't injecting you with Nanoprobes, but when you decide to allow others to control your destiny, the decision is being made for you. You're not choosing who you are or what you want out of life. In some way, which could be considered a form of assimilation.

Are you able to identify your Nemesis? For example, I mentioned earlier that I was shy. Whenever I started a new job, I would withdraw into my shell. Even though I had experience, I felt unsure of my abilities to perform the tasks. During my training, I sometimes felt I was being judged for not learning fast enough. I was intimidated when around those who knew their responsibilities and were efficient in doing them. I know that was my perspective as I was in my head. I could see being shy as my nemesis. What causes shyness? It could be rooted in intimidation, fear of rejection, or insecurities of some sort.

I had to identify why I was shy. When I thought back on my childhood, I remembered feeling like everyone around me was much bigger, surer of themselves, and outgoing. Psychology today also identifies these characteristics. I did not know then what I know now, I had to learn to become comfortable in my own skin. After a while, I began to express my interests around my peers more. I talked about my strengths and stop downplaying my talents and intelligence. As I gained confidence and interacted with more people, I realized I had a lot to offer to those in the world around me. I started to listen to myself and began to really like who I was. Another thing that really helped me over come shyness was refusing to allow anyone to take advantage of my children. I became their defender, but the bottom line is I faced it head on. There are still times when that nemesis tries to rear its ugly head, but I hate bullies and I saw that as bullying. As I listened more to what God's Word said about me, I was able to resist the urge to wear a mask or allow myself to be assimilated by blending in with conversation or attitude of my surroundings. I refused to allow shyness to assimilate me any longer. "I won't be…SHY!" Shyness to me was a mask that held me hostage in feeling intimidated, fearful, or insecure. But no more!

It takes grit to face your nemesis. I don't know what that looks like for you, but you do. Get a journal and write down your thoughts and feelings of what might be holding you back. Find out the masks you're wearing that may be empowering your nemesis and stomp it out! Do not allow yourself to be assimilated but instead take control over your world and choose liberty and freedom. This is your personal flag raised to launch your resistance.

My disclaimer is this could become a messy resistance in which you take on full responsibility for the battle you must wage. Before you can declare who, you are *not*, you must first know who you are. When you realize who you are… then, resistance is *not* futile!

IDENTITY THEFT

HAVE YOU EVER HAD ANYTHING STOLEN FROM you? An opportunity, a promotion, your peace of mind, your innocence, your dreams? The grooming process for your identity began as a child. Erikson says, "if we don't establish (ego) our self-image during adolescences, we struggle with who we are as adults." Yet, throughout generations we have learned to adapt to life situations. Yes, things have been stolen from us in our lifetime and we can simply accept it as just life. However, I believe we have a greater resilience within us to not just roll over and give up. While some did fall by the wayside, others accomplished their dreams achieving the imaginable in the arts, technology, medicine, law, politics, education, animation, and the list goes on.

So, let's define what it means to be a victim of identity theft. Let's use my scenario of the Borg in Star Trek Voyager. One of Janeway's nemesis is a single Borg by the name of Seven of Nine. She was assimilated at the age of six by the Borg collective who stripped from her every sense of self by the hive collective and forced on her a new identity. As Erikson stated, the ego must be established during adolescence, but she never had that opportunity because she was a Borg until adulthood. I watched her struggle with her identity even after she was rescued by Janeway. She didn't know if she was completely human or completely Borg or a mixture of both. She fought to get back what was stolen from her throughout the course of the series. Although this is an extreme example, people do struggle with self-identity. When you don't know who you are as a person, your gifts, talents, and abilities become assimilated into whatever the situation or circumstances dictate.

While technology made it more convenient to bank, pay our bills, keep contact with people for business and pleasure, it also made it easier to rob us of our identity through cybercrime theft. It's true we can lose our money, but our fight is for our sense of self and worth. Wikipedia defines identity theft as "when someone uses personally identifiable information such as your name, your date of birth, and your fingerprint." Just as in my example of the fictitious Borg, Seven of Nine's fight was being waged on the inside.

I am not exempt from the things that challenge my hopes and dreams just because I'm a believer in Jesus. There are inner battles I face every day just as you do. We wage the fight to maintain things we already possess and that includes the right to decide what kind of person we want to be. We should have the freedom to evolve into that person even if we're not sure what that may look like. That person is waiting to be discovered!

Let's not accept the images of the past telling you that you can't overcome the blows you've sustained which reinforced the strongholds that have prevented your dreams. What images are bound within your mind? Mark 3 and Matthew 12 say, in order to be robbed, the strong person must first be bound up, then their goods can be plundered. So, what images or words are bound within you while your hopes and dreams are plundered? Is it the memory of a past relationship that didn't survive the storms of life? Is it your body that has gained weight over the years that tells you that you'll never get it off or someone who told you you'll never amount to anything? God's Word could hold the answer for you as it says, "When the strong person is fully armed, they guard their possessions and keep them safe" (New International Version – UK, 1982, Luke 11:21).

To guard the possessions of your mind, you must be armed with a healthy perspective of life. It's okay to acknowledge the underdeveloped ego but grow beyond those negative experiences by looking for opportunities to rise and declare, I won't be a victim! I believe at some point we have been victimized in some way.

Still, I didn't raise these things to use as a blame game. We can choose to be a victim in life, or we can choose not to since we have access to resources right at our fingertips. What do you need to help you win the fight? Find it, ask someone for help, get into a program, apply for grants. Reach out to those who may have information that can help you.

I'm placing the responsibility back on you to make the changes necessary for your victory. This is your battle therefore, you must remember to take on full responsibility for the war you must wage. Pick up your sword of determination and swing it at the words that have wounded you. Cut asunder the past that has kept you hostage and remove the masks that told you that hiding is the only way you'll survive. Don't allow yourself to be robbed any longer by allowing your face and voice to be the perpetrators in your life.

Still, another strategy common with this thief is to convince us we can trust our negative emotions and feelings. These feelings tell us, this is who we are. It's good we have emotions because without them we wouldn't be human, but we don't have to allow them to run us.

Being controlled by emotions makes it's so easy to hide behind a mask. Just like positive emotions, negative emotions are the result of chemicals which are released in our brain. [3]"Feelings refer to the reactions that individuals have to external as well as internal factors. Emotions, on the other hand, refer to the internal factors." These eternal emotions are where the fight takes place. This is the battle ground of the mind where you win or lose. Dr. Carolyn Leaf stated in Switch on your Brain e-book pg. 52, "We are not victims to our biology. We are co-creators alongside

God. God leads, but we have to choose to let God lead. We have been designed to create thoughts, and from these we live out our lives" (Prov. 23:7).

To Be Seen

Everybody wants to be seen. Don't we? As I mentioned in the previous section about identity theft, we hide sometimes to protect ourselves from all the stuff that attempts to bury us. This is just as important to your resistance. Although we wear masks to hide the hurt, we want to be seen. When I started writing this chapter, I had to ask myself, "What does it mean to be seen?" After all I'm taking this journey with you. You'll have to answer this question for yourself as well. In the introduction of my book, "*Tent Master*," I mentioned, "We wander around in our situations clueless to just how needy we really are without the One who created us." This holds true for me especially when I feel broken by life situations. They have a way of bending you before the world and exposing your weaknesses.

"I need to be seen and heard by God who gives me hope to heal through my brokenness. I need to know He hears my silent tears. When I know He sees me, I don't feel judged but I'm instead able to reach out of my hurt and pain. Because I have experienced His love, I know He doesn't just hear my voice but my heart. It's like tears in a bottle, some of joy some of pain, like falling from the sky, counting drops when it rains, knowing all my ways, when I'm up when I'm down, not missing count of one, as they fall without a sound."

There are so many people who hurt in silence. They walk around wearing a mask that looks like them, but on the inside, they are crying out for help. The wonderful thing about God is he sees you in your pain and hears the rain drop of tears that flow without a sound. He's always present with His arms stretched out to save. All it takes is your asking Him for help.

To be seen means, it's okay to be me without pretense, without the mask because this is my haven. To be seen means, I don't have to disguise myself as a superhero when I need someone to be my superhero.

Love sees you. Love sees all of us. Although your story isn't the same as mine, it doesn't need to be. But for sure, you can embrace Him who sees you, He is here. He isn't just there for you but HERE, right where you are, even as you read these words.

He offers you His lovingkindness and tender mercies. "Behold, the eye of the Lord is upon them that fear Him, upon them that hope in His mercy;" (King James Version, 1604, Ps. 33:18). You don't have to be something you are not because He knows you already.

COMMUNICATION

COMMUNICATION IS IMPORTANT. ASK ALL THE TOP cell phone companies such as Verizon, AT&T, and T-Mobile. Yet, they don't have anything on the greatest communication device of all time, the heart. When we feel something stirring around within us, we let it out! When we hurt, we let you know about it. When we love, it comes from the heart and when we hate, it's there as well. So, here we have communication!

We are used to talking about what's going on in our lives. We talk to the therapist, best friends, hairdressers, and parents. I've read that, [4]"From the abundance of the heart, the mouth speaks." In this instance in the [5]Greek, heart is referred to as *kardía*, Kar-dee'-ah (soul or mind) which is where the center of our emotions lies. As we've learned in the previous chapters, our emotions can be good or bad, but our heart is from where we communicate what we feel. Now suppose we allow this center to be dominated by other's opinions. If so, here lies influence which we either accept or reject. Here lies our decision of whether to allow the negativity of society or social media to dictate to us how we should be or who we should be.

Again, suppose we take our heart to God and share with Him all the emotions that spew out of there. I believe it would have a more positive effect on our lives if we communicated with Him from that center. Why not talk with God about what's happening in our lives? How about if we decide to link ourselves with Him to a point that we arm ourselves and block those negative influences? However, to do that we must have a one-on-one dialog with Him. That's what prayer is, it's simply talking and listening. You know, it's a conversation where two or more people get to have their say. There is something about talking to God that can change worlds, not just the physical world but your world. So, think about using this strategy with someone bigger than you. This is yet another way to set up a resistance. It's your Tête-à-tête with God.

DECLARATION II
(WALK IT OUT)

I won't be,

Other people's plans, or dreams or talk

This life was given to me to walk

Tête-à-tête

Do you have a faith base? Religion is a big deal in America, it's a hot topic. America is known as the ⁶Melting Pot. This is a metaphor coined in 1708 for a fusion of nationalities, cultures, and ethnicities. So, you probably have different ethnicities running through your genes, which brought forth different belief systems and religions. Nowadays, companies such as Ancestry, 23 and me, etc., are capitalizing on testing your DNA to help you identify with your heritage.

Freedom of religion is the right of all Americans, it's our First Amendment. Where am I going with this? Well, how we view our religious beliefs could play a major role in how we walk life out. My faith is a moral barometer as my awareness of God's presence helps me to do the right thing. It's a part of my walk-in life. If my walk isn't a reflection of me, then the real me is hidden behind a mask. Although I place my confidence in my faith to help me make the right decisions, it's still my decision. My relationship with Jesus Christ helps define my standard of living. If I use His word as my guide, I have better success at achieving my goals. What standard do you use to guide your decision making?

Walk (Peripateō)

My hubby and I love to walk. We haven't done a marathon or anything of that sort but it's our time to talk to each other and catch up (while getting in those 10,000 steps). During our walks, we discuss our central focus. Where are we going in life? We discuss the method of transportation we'll use to get to our destination. This is the way we walk out our lives. When I say, "Walk" it's about the journey in life. My husband and I have a joint adventure as well as our individual goals but eventually, our plans intertwine. Still, our primary goal is to reflect Christ.

When we make decisions on how we want to walk, we're deciding how to live our lives. The Greek word *Peripateō* means, "to make one's way, progress; to make use of opportunities." The Hebrew word is, "to live, to regulate one's life, to conduct oneself as in morally." This is what it means to walk out your life. As I walk with the Lord, His Word is "A lamp for my feet, a light on my path" (New International Version, 1973, Ps. 119:105). I must humble myself, admit I need direction, and the Lord will lead me if I am willing to follow.

What's your center? Do you have a belief system? If you don't, maybe along the way you'll discover it. Here is an insert from psychiatrists and mental health counselors who use patient spirituality to help their mental health patients. This article is from [7]Psychology Today by Dr. Eugene Rubin M.D., Ph.D. who wrote, "It is difficult for psychiatrists to ignore the intersection of religion and medicine. Psychiatrists learn quickly about the belief systems that motivate an individual and work with these belief systems to assist a person in recovering from psychiatric illness." This suggests having a faith base can help with life situations.

This journal is about declaring who you are and building a strong self-image. A strong belief or faith system can in turn have a lot of influence on that image. Our flag of resistance needs help. We raise it as we arm ourselves with the right mind. However, the right mind must be equipped with an identity that can stand up against what others say about you.

The right influence can help you remain on the path of productivity, motivation, inspiration, and determination to get things done. Our walk is about our conversation. We want to present and conduct ourselves in a manner becoming of someone who wants positive outcomes in their lives. [8]"My child, listen and accept what I say [take in my speech.] Then you will have a long life [your years will be multiplied]" (Expanded Bible, 2011, Prov. 4:10). When I read this, I saw two things. One, I must actively listen, which means I take in what I'm hearing and decide how I want to use what I've heard. Two, I must accept what I've heard. By accepting what I've heard, I must agree with it and be willing to act upon it. Whether it's negative or positive advice, it will affect my decision making. Since this book is about resistance to things that might cause harm, maybe it can help promote healing by encouraging its readers to seek out someone with a positive influence. Do you have anyone in mind?

There are many positive people to emulate and good habits to adopt. There are people in your life and people of history to observe as a positive role model. There are people who have achieved their goals and made a great impression on your life. It could be your parents, siblings, best friend, mentors, spiritual leaders, and so on. So, you do not have to walk alone feeling as if you have no help because there are people who can help you. Can you think about who is in your life that has a positive influence on you enough to thrust you into the best version of yourself?

Your Walk is Uniquely You!

I love watching old black and white movies. Thanks Mom! They have an appeal to me and a uniqueness that keep my imagination engaged and the wheels in my mind turning. They bring out the authenticity of life without polluting or solving it. It leaves the decision making to the observer for me. It is also where the uniqueness lies in my opinion. There are no special effects, just raw life with the challenges that come. Our uniqueness comes out in those challenges as life helps bring out who we are capable of being and what we can do.

Whoever you are, you are exclusive. Every facet of your design is handmade, not man-made. Yet, holding on to who you are will be met with some resistance to stay the course. There will be pressure to accept what the latest fad may be or temptation to be sidetracked to take a different path. Most often, life is not just a straight walk. A lot of the times, life zig zags. Even having a clear path from knowing what you want out of life usually will come with some bumps in the road. Still, who better to light the way for you than the One who formed and shaped you in your mother's womb? He knows and understands every print you will make in your lifetime.

Your uniqueness shouldn't be smothered beneath other's thoughts, ideas, and desires. That is why it's so important to be confident and love who you are. It's okay if you're not perfect at everything. It is okay if you don't dress in the latest fashion. Make your own statement by being unique. Start your own fashion, you be the trend setter. The way you talk, walk, and see life is unique. Your smile and laugh are unique. I think you get the point. As simple as that sounds, that is what makes you, you.

The smallest things can bring a smile to someone's face. Here is a short story for you. One winter my job was having a sale on specialty items. Well, I stopped by the vendor and saw this cute pink bunny hat that I gave to my daughter, and she wears that bunny hat faithfully. She pulls Bunny out at the first sign of cold weather. Whenever she wears it, people stop her to say how her smile and that hat made them smile. That quirky hat and her smile made a difference to someone else. The simplest things in life can make a difference. I believe you can touch other's lives with what you have to offer but if you hide your quirkiness behind a mask trying to be someone else, who's going to be you? Your uniqueness can touch people like no one else can. There are things that you do that no one else can do. No one can walk your walk or talk your talk, it's yours, so own it!

DECLARATION III
(Bust A Move)

I won't be,

Some side order waiting for a second chance

I will make my own music, dance my own dance

TÊTE-À-TÊTE

It's time to sit and talk about you. How are you doing? What changes if any, have you made since reading this book? This book is about you. It's about removing pretense (masks) and being real. It's about your potential to be successful in your endeavors to reach your goals and be happy with yourself and your life. Your imagination and ingenuity are revved up! Let's put it to good use.

The Rut Stops Here

There may be times, despite your best efforts, that you may get stuck in a rut. It can feel something like the hamster on the wheel that gets you moving but you're going nowhere. So, what can be done to get off the wheel? It will require you to think about what you want to do with this gift called life. I remember the times I've felt that way. I ask myself, "What is it that I am passionate about? What is it that I care about the most?" Well, I thought about all the dreams I've had. I went back as far as I could remember and thought about my dreams as a child. I thought to myself, "What is the thing(s) that has stuck with me even into my adulthood?" Writing! I remembered leaving poems on the bathroom mirror for my mom to read when she got up for work every morning. There were other things, but writing has weathered them all. So, the next time you feel like you're on that hamster wheel, just do a little reminiscing.

Procrastination

Procrastination will kill a good idea. Waiting on just the perfect moment, season, or event will dry out your enthusiasm. Next thing you know, you're taking on what's leftover. Anytime you second guess what you want, you settle for the side orders of life. How often do you take a chance? How many times have you talked yourself out of it? Albert Einstein is famously credited with saying, "The definition of insanity is doing the same thing over and over again but expecting different results." Life is full of first chances however, you may need to change your routine. Challenge yourself to think outside of the norm. Take the first step, you need to start somewhere. Bust a move and see where it leads you. If you have breath, then you have the opportunity. The only person that can stop you is you.

Procrastination makes one lazy with the leftovers of, "if only." Seize the day, and learn the lesson of the Ant.

"Oh, Lazy Sluggard"

I Won't Be!

Oh, lazy sluggard, the winds will come to call you in to stay, but you don't hear the howling wind cause you just want to play, the ants all know what time it is and work to have their meal, but lazy sluggard will not work your stomach you not fill.

The ant is wise consider his ways and learn what he has done. He filled his home with lots of food for winter is to come. Heed the acts that lead him on, no chief or ruler say,

"Winter comes to pluck it out, no time for you to play, go gather what you might, for soon, winter is on its way,"

He knows his job, he quickly puts all crumbs, sweets, and nooks, adds cakes and pie, McDonald fries, all legal, he's no crook. Gather lunch, breakfast, dinner; take it back with cheer, even sip a little honey, for wintertime is near.

But you O' sluggard fat in summer, fall is soon about, there will be no fun or laughter for you, but hunger from the drought.

Oh, lazy sluggard winds will come, to call you in to stay, but you don't hear the howling wind cause you just want to play, the working man or ants who dance, happy cupboards filled, they're all warm sing and prance, while sorry sluggard chilled, "Winter came, took my meat, I had my fun, no more to eat."

The ants all know what time it is and work to have their meal, but lazy sluggard did not work your stomach you not fill.

Appetizer or Main Dish

You know when you go to your favorite restaurant and the waiter comes to your table and asks, "Would you like something to drink or like to order an appetizer while you wait for the main dish?" You sit at your table, eat the appetizers, and sometimes get full. Then, when the real meal arrives, you're not as hungry. When you get full on the appetizer, you have no room for the main dish. You gave your hunger over to the appetizers. It's not there to fill you up, but to eat just enough until the main dish arrives.

When you settle, you miss out on opportunities. The next thing you know, you're working on other people's ideas and dreams instead of your own. Those are opportunities that should be yours. Don't convince yourself or let anyone else convince you that you can't obtain your dreams. Helping someone else accomplish their dreams is noble but that will not help you achieve your own. I think it's fine to want to help others fulfill their dreams but not at the cost of sacrificing your own plans. If you're sitting on the sideline watching others, time is chipping away your energy, motivation, and creativity that you should be investing in yourself. Please don't do that to yourself. Instead, put in the work it will take for you to be successful.

Appetizers are yummy but you may need to skip and go straight for the main dish. Appetizers are the coming attractions, but the main dish is why you sat down at the table. There is plenty for everyone at the table of success. Your appetite for life will help create as many chances to succeed as you need. Besides, you were never created to be second to anything or anyone. You have your own goals to accomplish. Don't settle! Push yourself until you see your dreams and desires come to fruition.

Don't try to hold every single aspect of your dreams and goals in your head. It may be helpful to take a moment to write them down as putting them in writing can help you to become organized. When you see what you want, you are more determined to successfully go after it. This is something I've been learning to be consistent at doing. I'm telling you; it makes such a difference! I've read over ideas and goals that I've wanted to accomplish which helped me from deviating from my plans. I also got a vision for my life as I wrote them down. Wisdom says, "Write the vision and make it plain on tablets, that he may run who reads it" (New King James Version, 1969, 2003, Hab. 2:2). You need to catch your vision. I've learned to practice making both short-term and long-term goals. I also know this is something that successful business professionals and career counselors advise.

Also, don't allow discouragement to derail you. Sometimes the plans you make may not turn out as you'd hoped but that doesn't mean they weren't good plans. Just rethink them. Were they obtainable? If not, go back and break it down into subsections so that you can make them as specific as possible. If a plan isn't working out, then decide if that's the right way to go about it. Then, if you believe it's right for you, do the research and find others who have similar ideas who have achieved their goals. Most importantly, don't give up on your dreams.

DECLARATION IV (RUN THIS RACE)

I won't be stopped, quit or

lose my place

There's a prize for me

In this human race

TÊTE-À-TÊTE

So here you are again. You are building up a resistance against those things that would try to rob you of your identity. Can you see the masks falling by the wayside? The you that you were born to be is gradually being unveiled. You are waging a good fight and I'm honored you decided to read this book as a step towards strengthening your resistance to help launch you forward in your race. I hope reading this book so far has shown you some strategies on how to keep the resistance alive. You must keep building your immune system to increase your stamina. Stay motivated in your investment.

Visualize yourself running this race. The sweat is like a torrential downpour on your face and back, but you can see the progress you've made. You must keep moving! Make steady strides to keep the pace so you can have enough energy to reach the finish line. This race isn't for the faint of heart. This race takes guts and grit. Think about what it cost you to get this far. Don't give up! Dig in and Run this Race!

RUN THIS RACE!

ONE OF THE THINGS YOU SHOULD KEEP IN MIND about this race is it's yours. This life is yours to decide how you want to live it and what you want to do with it. You're not running against anyone but yourself. That's why you must know who you are and what you want out of life. Again, this is your race. You set the goals, you set the pace, you decide what kind of race, and you determine whether you succeed. There will be challenges but they are meant to be overcome.

When you declare what you will or will not be, you set the tone. There have been times when I look at my vision journal and thoughts come up like, do you think you can do that? Yes, I also have a vision journal. It helps me to keep my eyes on the prize. I have written God's promises in my journal to remind me of what He promised. His Word is a written contract. I also use pictures that reflect my race to help me keep my vision always before my eyes. In front of my vision journal, I have these written words, [9]"Write the vision and make it plain." I keep it right where

I look at it every day and be reminded of what my race is about. I pray, read, and meditate over it. That is a part of how I run my race. Your race will look different, but you should always keep your vision before your eyes. There is a saying that goes, "Out of sight out of mind." Keeping your vision before your eyes helps when you have those days when you question if it's possible to do. Walt Disney said, "If you can dream it, you can do it." My question to you is, how big can you dream?

This race is also about self-discipline. That means you must push yourself beyond your feelings, emotions, and even your weaknesses despite obstacles to pursue what you want and achieve your goals. I know some things will challenge you such as procrastination and sometimes being stuck in a rut. Fatigue can set in making you feel emotionally drained. Step back and take a breather. You need to stay motivated to run this race. So, while you're reviewing your goals, remind yourself why you want what you want because this race is about you. Don't allow the bumps along the way to move you from your place.

Your Place in Life

Your place in life is important, for you are positioned to connect with others throughout your journey. Your connection with others will make just as much of an impact on them as their connections will with you. The business lingo is to have, "a book of business." These are the people with whom you connect that may offer something to help you accomplish your goals just as you help them accomplish theirs while pressing forward.

Since we are running our own Olympic race, the quest for our gold is still ahead of us. Let's pinpoint the details and specifics of our race. Pay attention to the steps we've made so that we don't lose our place. We should be purposeful about how to accomplish our dreams and plans. I was listening to a minister preach who mentioned, "We have stopped dreaming. We've allowed the enemy to steal our dreams." Consider any mountain that blocks the path to finish the race an enemy. Our dreams fuel our vision, or our vision gives fuel to our dreams. Either way, if we stop dreaming or visualizing what we want to accomplish, we will have lost something valuable that greatly contributes to our success in life. Our place in life isn't just geographical, but mental, and emotional as well. Where are you in your head? How are you thinking about your goal and mentally planning for it to happen? I agree with Bishop TD Jakes who once preached on the power of a thought, "So if a corporation is not a product and it's not a person, and it's not a premise, not property, what is a corporation literally? It's a thought. Do you have the courage to think? Because if you can think, you can change, you can move, you can evolve, you can grow, you can become, you are one IDEA away." Therefore, whatever your endeavor, it's just a thought away!

Hold Your Peace

I GET EXCITED ABOUT MY DREAMS AND VISION while I'm running my race. Not everyone is privy to my dreams. I have a few select friends and family with whom I share who will encourage and support me in my race. Unfortunately, not everyone will believe what I want to do is even possible. It can be the same with you because not everyone will believe you can turn your life around, achieve your goals, be successful, and rip off the masks of pretense. Sad to say, not everyone wants you to be successful. However, keep those at a minimum who do offer support for your race and your dreams.

You have a personal crown to obtain. No matter how small your goal seems, it's a building block to the next step. The crown you want to obtain is the crown of achievements. Your goal could be to get your high school diploma or G.E.D., maybe no one else in your family has gotten theirs and you'll be the first. Maybe you want to get a college degree, start your own business, be a successful published author as I do, lose weight, or be rehabilitated from an addiction. No matter how big or small, these desires are important to you because they represent your crown to obtain. I don't know where this book will find you but one thing of which I am sure, you are worth it! As you go through your process, let people observe and be amazed at the outcome. Next thing you know, you're the one they'll ask, "How did you do it?"

Tête-à-Tête

I ADDED THIS TÊTE-À-TÊTE ON PURPOSE BECAUSE I want you to take a moment to evaluate where you are in your race. Here amid trying to accomplish what may seem impossible goals, bumps or obstacles can threaten to block your efforts. Obstacles may seem impossible to get past like immovable mountains. Mountains are good object lessons because they represent something that's bigger than us. Although they appear to be immovable, whatever mountain you're facing can be overcome. You must be determined that no matter the barriers nor strongholds blocking your view, you will find a way to get past them.

I'm adamantly unyielding when it comes to my success. Why? Because it's you and it's me! When other's see you overcome difficult situations to accomplish your dreams, they will believe it's possible for them to accomplish theirs also. Mary, Mary, Gospel Record Artists, have a song entitled, "Go Get It!" The verse I like says, "If you wanna get what you never got, you gotta do something you never done." Most of the time, things we want to do we've never done before. It's like treading uncharted waters. We might start off not sure in which direction to go, but as we develop a plan things start to come together. Since this race is yours, run it in such a way that it will leave no doubt to spectators that all things are possible.

Mountain Mover

I WANT TO START OFF BY DECLARING, "YOU ARE A mountain mover. A force to be reckoned with!" Declare that over yourself. Mahalia Jackson sang, "Lord don't move my mountain but give me the strength to climb." I believe we need strength to endure challenges that may take a little more time to overcome. Mountains that challenge your endurance are not easy to ignore. They challenge our faith, our tenacity, and our resolve. Obstacles can push us to strive for better or cause our defeat. This song is inspirational and uplifting and has helped us look to God for strength. However, can I tell you mountains that block your way aren't meant to be climbed but instead to be commanded to move out of the way! Can you believe it is possible to move the impossible? So, what can we do to get past mountain-like obstacles? It's written "Truly I tell you, if anyone says to this mountain, 'Go, throw yourself into the sea,' and does not doubt in their heart but believes that what they say will happen, it will be done for them," (NIV 1973, Mark 11:23)! Do we need to move a literal mountain? Probably not, but the point is, if we have faith we can move a literal mountain, then we have faith to believe we can move mountain like obstacle blocking our success in life.

One of the ways I make demanding situations in my life move is to engage in praise and worship. Through praise and worship, I am able to move the mountain of thoughts that tell me it's impossible. I'm able to walk in faith with confidence that this race isn't impossible to win.

Don't just speak to the thing that's blocking your path, but also speak to your dreams and tell them to wake up within you. No matter how many obstacles are still blocking your path, speak to them and command them to move! They can appear in many ways. It could be something in your mind or way of thinking that has held you captive. It could be a mountain of debt that's been preventing you from being credit worthy to buy a home. Maybe, you've lost a loved one and you're going through a mountain of emotions that says, "you'll never get over that feeling of loss." I remember the mountain of emotions I experience when my parents passed. I don't care how old you are, it hurts to lose them. I remember feeling orphaned and alone, but God's Word says, "He will never leave you nor forsake you," (NIV 1973 Deuteronomy 31:6,8; Hebrews 13:5). It took a lot for me to speak God's Word to that mountain of hopelessness and depression, but I did, "I am not alone. God my Father has not forsaken me!" I kept speaking to that mountain and it did obey. I have so much joy and hope that I will see them again. Why? Because I read in the book of Exodus 3:6, 15; Mark 12:27 that, I don't serve a God of the dead but of the living. What are the mountains you are supposed to command? I told you how I do it. Do you want to try? Remember, you are a mountain mover, a force to be reckoned with!

We know that struggles happen in life, but they don't have to define your future because you're a mountain mover and a force to be reckoned with. Sometimes mountains can bring out the worst or best in us but allow the latter. I've sat down and faced some difficult situations having to decide to give up or get up. I chose the latter. Sometimes when you get tired of losing, crying, or giving in, that's your moment of decision. My friend, I want you to do more than just survive but more importantly to overcome! Remember, you are "a mountain mover, a force to be reckoned with!" Even if you've failed and the voice in your head tells you to quit, recall hearing my voice telling you, "You've got what it takes for you're a mountain mover and force to be reckoned with!"

DECLARATION V
(Perseverance)

It may seem darkest before the sunrise

Armed and dressed for the battle

I will rise!

It may seem darkest before the sunrise
Armed and dressed for the battle
I will rise!

TÊTE-À-TÊTE

It's time for a pep talk. Let's take a breather and just chill. Get a cup of coffee or tea (I'm a big tea drinker) and just look back on your life. As I think back to the beginning of this journey, I want to thank you for coming this far with me. To think that someone else has been reading this journal and becoming familiar with who you are is amazing to me because that's what this journey has produced in me. I've learned a lot about myself through this process of gaining confidence and guts to take my stand against negativity regardless of where it comes. I want to have a joyful and fulfilled life.

There have been times that I've gotten tired emotionally and mentally even as I write this book, but I want these words to matter. I pray more they help you in some way to find your niche, your thing, or your purpose as you read with me. Although I haven't seen your face or heard your voice, I feel you're with me. My heart and my love go out to you. I pray that by the time you finish this book, you will have metamorphosed into the beautiful, creative, amazing person you were born to be. Don't let anything stop you from achieving your dreams. I'm rooting for you!

It's a Fight Worth Fighting

Declaring what you will or will not tolerate is a battle worth the fight. It's worth scrapping to become who you want to be. It's worth standing against the opposition that *tries* to define you. You see, we have the right to choose in which direction we want our lives to go be it good or bad. God has given us a will and a right. The Declaration of Independence reads, "We hold these truths to be self-evident, that all men are created equal, that they are endowed by their Creator with certain unalienable Rights that among these are Life, Liberty and the pursuit of happiness." Whether the persons who wrote this believed it for all people or not, these rights belong to you. How many of us believe in our God-given right to be happy and to pursue our dreams? If everyone believed this for his neighbor, there wouldn't be such a fight in the ability for them to live out that right.

Now, I'm not going to get into equal rights here because we've seen in history, even today, that some rights are not always equal. Yet, this is one of the reasons we fight to obtain our life, liberty, and the pursuit of happiness. We already know things aren't just going to be handed over to us. Therefore, we must be determined to will ourselves to get it done. As stated in the movie *Mission Impossible*, "Your mission, should you choose to accept it," is to fight for you. We can't allow ourselves to become prey to an unhealthy lifestyle that controls us such as addictions, toxic relationships, mindsets, or eating habits. Therefore, arm yourself with the mission, for the mission is, you!

BE EMPOWERED WITH THE RIGHT MOTIVE

We know that in life sometimes stuff happens causing us to miss the mark. When I started this book, I set some personal goals for myself. I wanted to be at my ideal weight and size before the end of summer. I started this plan at the beginning of the year. I wrote down the amount of weight I wanted to lose and had an exercise regimen in place. Well, I didn't meet my goal and actually I missed it altogether. When I looked at what I had written down, it was a sound and reachable goal, but I still missed the mark. I was upset with myself over it. I could have fallen into the blob of feeling like I'm a failure.

Then, I realized this was an opportunity to rethink what I had written. Failure is something I believe can empower you. Why do I believe that? I believe it because I had another chance to decide if I went about it the right way. I had to ask myself why I was doing it? What was my motive? For whom was I doing it? Was I doing it for health reasons? Did I like myself? Do I feel attractive to my husband? These were tough questions I had to answer before I could reset my goals. The bottom line for me was to be healthy. So, I set new goals with that in mind. I empowered myself with the right motive to stay focused. I became more aggressive and less passive. So, just because you don't succeed the first time, try it again because you are worth it.

DECLARATION VI (Grit)

Standing up, I'm all about it

I'll fight my way through

times seem down

I won't give in

Anything less than that, won't do!

Standing up,
I'm all about it
I'll fight my way through
times seem down
I won't give in
Anything less just
won't do!

Tête-à-Tête

Hello! It's you again. I wonder if things seem a little heated at some stage of your progress. If so, then that's good. That means you are facing obstacles and may have even had some setbacks. Keep it moving. Keep the vision before your eyes. Since you've been reading this book, what techniques have you developed to help you move forward? What new strategies have you invented to push you beyond the challenges? What new weapons have you compiled to resist giving up? What new allies have you enlisted? Think about all the things, people, and techniques you've devised and fire all your ammunition at the resistance.

You're on your way and you must win the battle to stay on course for your healing, wholeness, and success in achieving your goals and dreams. That weight won't come off without a plan. That addiction won't be conquered without the right program suited for you and exercise of your will to overcome it. Those negative emotions and thoughts may resist change but remain steadfast in gaining your peace of mind. It's going to take GRIT!

TRUE GRIT

MY MOM LOVED WATCHING JOHN WAYNE movies. So naturally, I grew up liking his movies too. One of the movies I liked is *"True Grit."* His character was a one-eyed Marshall and Texas ranger by the name of Rooster Coburn. He'd been doing bounty hunting his entire life. Grit is what it took to chase down the fugitives of the old west.

Grit is the resolve to persevere despite challenges. We need to possess perseverance which is defined as a continued effort to do. It is the act of achieving something despite difficulties, failure, or opposition, it's the action or condition or an instance of persevering: steadfastness. It will take all of that to resist anything that would hinder your dreams. I've inserted this powerful exultation, "And let us not grow weary while doing good, for in due season we shall reap if we do not lose heart" (New King James Version, 1982, Gal. 6:9). This scripture is immensely powerful. We know there will be days when we might grow tired of constantly pushing ourselves as we continue to pursue our goals. Sometimes we may become emotionally and mentally tired. However, if we don't give up, we will reap the reward of seeing our hard work manifest. I hope you don't mind that I put that little nugget in there. Be encouraged!

Your dreams come with a cost. It cost sweat and tears, time and effort, determination, endurance, and consistency. You must have the grit to endure the opposition that may or shall I say will come against you. As Debbie Allen stated in the movie *Fame*, "You want fame? Fame cost and right here is where you pay." Do you want your dreams and goals fulfilled and to be a success? Don't grow weary in well-doing!

Arise!

As you read this section, think about a situation that has kept you from meeting your full potential in a particular area. Think about the struggle you are currently dealing with right now. What situations are you dealing with that require you to rip off the mask of falsity? Does it define you or make you doubt your true identity? Pinpoint what's hindering you from arising out of that situation.

Now, let's define arise. One of the Greek meanings for arise is "To become empowered, to stand, to maintain oneself, to endure." Webster dictionary uses, "To move upward, to ascend." When we go through difficult situations, the struggle is real. It's a struggle first in the mind to keep it safe from outer influences. When we must deal with adverse situations, we must maintain our resolve to move upward in our thinking. We must ascend above negativity. An example of a low thought could be, "You'll never reach your goals. You'll never break free of that addiction; you'll never rise above depression." You must work your plan to arise from that low thought. You must therefore have a strategy in place. The battle is, to resist taking the low thought. The opposition you face is always personal first because it's starts with a thought. We must bring the fight to the street of our minds. I have probably said it before, this is where the battle is won or lost. When you stand your ground and refuse to give up, you empower yourself. You begin to reach for those creative ideas, go to people who have wrestled and won, ask for help, and confide in only those who will push you to be the best version of yourself.

I told you that I love old movies. Well, I also like to take a few pointers from movies such as, "*Unsinkable Molly Brown*" played by Debbie Reynolds. One of my favorite quotes in the movie is when she makes it clear, "Nothing will keep me down until I say I'm down." That's strong! We can arise above whatever tries to keep us down. However, we must decide to rise and not sink under the pressure. We are empowered when we have the right mind to plow through the things that try us.

Let's dig deep within and determine to arise! I can't spell out what those situations might be for you because I don't know what they are, but you do. If it's something that can hinder your success, then wage your war against it. Remember my disclaimer? This could become a messy resistance in which you take on full responsibility for the battle you must wage." You take responsibility to finish what you started. Don't give up!

Another heavy-duty weapon that can help you arise is hope. A situation, enemy or person can dismantle your hope and stop you from believing you can win. However, you can calm the raging thoughts and wrong ideas with hope. Be meticulous about where you place your hope.

So, what is this weapon of hope? "To look forward to with desire and reasonable confidence, to believe, desire, or trust." When you watch television, read newspapers, magazines, and social media so many people lose hope for life. Hope can be the foundation that gives people the confidence to live one more day, to fight one more battle, or to strive to stay in the race.

A person with no hope sounds like this, "Why are you in despair, O my soul? And why are you restless and disturbed within me?" (Amplified Bible, 2015, Ps. 43:5) That is a description of someone who has lost hope. They are depressed and breaking down from within. Their mind and emotions have collapsed beneath the pressure. In other words, someone or something has dismantled their inner strength to the point they stopped functioning from within. You know a good fight when you see one so you're not that person. This fight is rigged if you use this arsenal and point it at the low thought.

My living hope is Christ within me. He is living and active within my world, my inner self, and my being. I've quickly come to the realization that when the battle ensues and tries to overtake me, I can't depend on just me or place total dependence in other people. There are things beyond me that I can't handle. I need power, ability, and strength to soar above the things that would try to hold me back. Therefore, I place my desires, reasonable confidence, and trust in Christ. If you don't have this hope, it's available to you. It's free of charge.

If you feel you've lost hope for this race, ask yourself a few questions like, "Am I depending on just myself and my resources? Did I miss doing something that could have helped move my goals forward? Do I need to change my way of thinking about some things? Have I taken the low thought? What have I put my reasonable confidence in?" Another thing don't write anything in stone. Allow changes to come naturally. Don't be impatient with yourself but allow the process to take place. Try to enjoy the process. That may sound strange but, on the way, to seeing your dreams come true, you must enjoy the process as well. It shouldn't be drive, drive, drive until it's done. Don't get lost in the process but remember, this is your life and it's meant to be enjoyed. One last thing, keep your declaration on your lips. "I won't be…?"

You ever thought of laughter as a weapon? I love a good laugh. My youngest son always spends time together with me in the kitchen while I'm preparing dinner. We have the most entertaining conversations. He leaves me in stitches with some of the stuff he comes up with. Well, I read that, "a cheerful heart is good like medicine" (NIV 1973 Proverbs 7:22). There have been days when a good laugh after work shook off all the cares of the day. Laughing helps to change my mood. Things don't seem so bleak after I have had a good laugh. According to the expert's laughter changes the chemicals in your brain. There is an article published by Harvard University T.H Chan of Public Health that tells us negative emotions can harm the body, [10]"Serious, sustained stress or fear can alter biological systems in a way that, over time, adds up to "wear and tear" and, eventually, illnesses such as heart disease, stroke, and diabetes. Chronic anger and anxiety can disrupt cardiac function by changing the heart's electrical stability, hastening atherosclerosis, and increasing systemic inflammation. But laughter can help to create a healthy body. Psychology today reads, [11]"Although laughter is not generally under voluntary control, it has numerous health benefits. Bouts of laughter can boost the immune system, relax muscles aid circulation, and protect against heart disease. It can abet metal health too; laughter can lower anxiety; releases tension improve mood can foster resilience."

[12]US Department Veterans Affairs also supports," Laughter has physiological effects; it changes body chemistry and brain function. Laughter increases heart and respiratory rates as well as oxygen consumption over a short period." These articles give good reason that laughter is a good weapon to combat negative emotions that can negatively affect our wellbeing.

Sometimes life is serious but there is joy and laughter as well. Take time out to focus on things that can bring cheerfulness and comedy to promote a healthy wellbeing.

I Won't Be!

Let's give ourselves a fighting chance to rise above situations that want to keep us down. Put on a funny movie and laugh your way to a healthy successful life!

DECLARATION VII
(Humility)

There may be tears and pain along the way,

But I know who I am,

On my knees, I will pray

There may be tears and pain along the way,
I know who I am,
On my knees, I will pray

Tête-à-Tête

Whew! Can I be transparent with you? I'm a little tired. Do you know what I realize about myself when I'm tired? It's easy to give up and just quit. It's easy to just throw in the towel. When I'm tired, I lose my focus. Have you ever felt like that? Sometimes my mind just shuts down. I don't want to think about whether I've reached my goals, push myself to continue with this dream, or even make efforts to resist. Sometimes it's necessary to humble myself to admit I need help.

It takes a lot to arise from hurt, pain, and disappointments. It takes courage to rip off the masks of pretense and uncover the real you. It takes a lot to resist the urge to hide behind a mask which you have made your haven. It takes a lot to recover from people's damaging words and disapproval of you. Most people want approval from loved ones and close friends to the extent they will do anything to get it. Why? Possibly to avoid rejection and disapproval from the people they most admire. However, when you try to meet other's expectations you sometimes fail yourself. What I hope you see regarding yourself is, you're enough! Even if people don't get you, you're enough. If they don't notice your accomplishments, you're still enough. Any brokenness you may have endured doesn't have to be permanent. Start visualizing your wholeness and let's keep it moving. Your greatest battle will eventually be your greatest victory!

Your Greatest Battle

It takes so much energy to see your dreams and plans come together and to remain persistent in the face of slammed doors and no, no, no. Still, keep pushing onward. Fuel up for your resistance by committing to yourself you'll see this through to the end. Keep aiming all your artillery at the opposition. Then, before you know it, you will have gained leverage, things will start to come together, and whoosh! You get it done. Victory! Hooray! You celebrate and then, RELAX. You take off your armor, put down your sword and shield, and BAM! Something else pops up. Oh no! Yet, you're physically and emotionally exhausted.

You've given all you had to win the last battle. Now you must put the armor of determination back on, raise your shield of resistance again, accept you have no more energy left to fight because you spent it all on the last battle, but still you fight. Your greatest battle lies before you. Sometimes you may feel you don't have enough strength to win another battle. The last one took everything you had to stand against the opposition.

One of my husband's favorite authors was Dr. Edwin Cole, the founder of Christian Men's Network and author of books such as *Communication, Sex, and Money*, and *Maximized Manhood* who wrote, "Your greatest battle is the eve of your victory." The eve of your victory is after you've celebrated and relaxed. The party poppers are still on the floor, the cake still on the table, and melted ice cream in the bowls but you've been called to another battle and all your strength is spent.

I like the slogan from Dry Idea deodorant commercial that goes, "Never let them see you sweat!" I used to say that to myself when I needed to be tough in a difficult situation. I didn't want anyone to know when I was afraid or hurting inside. I didn't want to let anyone see the dent in my armor from when life had beaten me up. What I didn't realize then but realize now is that I was strengthened in humbling myself rather than fighting my battles alone. I needed to allow someone to help me. My greatest champion is my Savior Jesus Christ, so on my knees I will pray.

Prayer is my greatest weapon against pride because in prayer, I must bow my heart and acknowledge I have a need that I cannot supply. I must also trust in a power that I cannot see with my natural eyes and believe in what I cannot physically hold on to. In my book, *Tent Master*, "Faith in the Midst," I found an awesome quote that expresses when you're out of answers to life dilemmas written from *The Treasury of Prayers* by B.M. Bound. It states, "In the study of prayer, of its activities and enterprises, the first place must of necessity be given to faith. It is the initial quality in the heart of any man who essays to talk to the Unseen. He must out of sheer helplessness, stretch forth hands in faith. He must believe, where he cannot prove." We naturally look for a physical experience that our senses can relate to but the mystery of answered prayer doesn't always appeal to our natural senses. This is where desperate hearts pray to the Unseen to grasp for answers to be revealed. My heart has been there many times where I've had to humble myself and believe in prayer where I could not prove. This is where my insufficiency is uncovered. Pride can keep anyone from receiving for it cannot coexist with humility. The difference I've found between the two is pride will bring you low, but humility will raise you up to believe in the unseen. "Eye have not seen, nor ear heard, nor have entered into the heart of man, the things which God has prepared for those who love Him" (New King James Version Bible pub yr.,1982, 1 Cor. 2:9).

When we try to fight the elements of life in our strength, we quickly discover we need some serious help. When I cry out to Him, He will lift me. "For wherever I am, though far away at the ends of the earth, I will cry to you for help. When my heart is faint and overwhelmed, lead me to the mighty, towering Rock of safety" (The Living Bible, 1971, Ps. 61:2).

I Won't Be!

I bow my heart before His presence, and I am refreshed and renewed. He gives me new strength to continue to pursue my hopes and dreams. My strength is renewed because I inquire of Him. I ask Him for direction, and I ask Him for help. I know that I can't live this life without Him. This is the key to my goals, dreams, and plans. Where does your strength lie? Where or to whom can you go to be refueled from life's battles? Give it some thought.

DECLARATION VIII
(The Beauty of You)

I'm proud and beautiful been set free

Anything less than who I am

I Won't Be!

Tête-à-tête

Here we are, almost at the end of the book, but the resistance continues until you no longer need to pretend, until you are enough, until the masks have fallen away. Here is a time to reflect on the journey. This last stanza wraps up the entire declaration. Being proud of who you are will bring out the beauty of what you are. This beauty isn't make-up that you buy from the store to enhance your outward appearance, it's the make-up of you. It's what life helped put together, the good and the bad. How have you adorned yourself with your experiences? What gifts were born out of necessity? How have you handled trials and challenges that came your way? Despite the pain of hardships, they birth either the will to push beyond them or tendency to fall prey to them. My hope is that even if you've had moments that you fell prey to challenges, they weren't the end of your story. You're not done with you yet.

Your beauty is first within. If you look deep enough, you'll see there is much about which to be proud. I don't mean proud as in puffed up or arrogant but happy with what you have done, achieved, or even survived. You must have faced something in your life that made you lift your head up high. Perhaps something in this book opened your eyes to a whole new person within that you didn't know existed.

This moment right here is where the façade ends. This moment right here is where the faults, shortcomings, and mistakes are accepted, and you move forward. Either you take them as your teachers, learn from the lessons, pass the tests, or remain on step one afraid to take on the challenges and overcome them. I'm betting you'll muster up all the grit inside and allow life to teach you just how amazing you really are. Break free from the old and walk into the new. Does that sound like a cliché? Maybe. But it's possible.

Don't be less, don't dummy down to anything less than what you want to be or do with yourself. God knows the frame of your moving parts. He knows how life has shifted you from one season to another. He's walked the journey of this poem, to help you strip away the masks that have kept you hidden. As for me, I couldn't do it alone and I still can't. I haven't arrived because I'm still growing and learning. I still walk out this bold declaration, whether I'm confident or feeling intimidated by things life brings across my path. Yet, I walk with the help of my Savior Jesus Christ.

I'm proud and beautiful because Jesus is the beauty that dwells within me. It is written, "[13]But we have this treasure in earthen vessels, that the excellence of the power may be of God and not of us." (New King James Version, 1982, 2 Cor. 4:7). It is His power by which I have been set free. To declare anything less than who I am would say, Christ in me is less. That's impossible because He raises me to be who He is. I like what Edna Mode from the Incredibles stated, "I don't look back because it distracts me from the now." The most important thing I can do is to keep my focus, [14]"I set the Lord always before me; Because He is at my right hand I shall not be moved," (New King James Version, 1982, Ps. 16:8), that way I know I can achieve whatever I put my mind to do.

The Philosophies of Past Heroes

God created us as His perfect work and His hands fashioned us to overcome life's obstacles. We are handmade, not man-made, a mysterious design from our Master craftsman's mind; a compilation of His love to stand the test of time.

The beauty of you can stand tall, shoulders straight, heads high. The beauty of you is ingrained in the trails blazed by heroes gone before you. It's these amazing philosophies that are a part of our makeup. A part of my make up is the identity which lies in a strong history of activism which has paved the way for my freedom as demonstrated by [15]Dr. Martin Luther King Jr. He didn't believe in giving up no matter what you wanted to do with your life. He said, [16]" Be a bush if you can't be a tree. If you can't be a highway, just be a trail. If you can't be a sun, be a star. For it isn't by size that you win or fail. Be the best of whatever you are."

Educator Dorothy Height, who was president of the National Council of Negro Women for 40 years, said, "Greatness is not measured by what a man or woman accomplishes but by the opposition he or she has overcome to reach his goals." These are our heroes, and we can't allow them to go to sleep in our memories. A part of the *I Won't Be* declaration is about wrestling with the opposition that wants to keep us from fulfilling our dreams. The thread of determination has been woven into us, the only thing that's left is to activate it. I thank God for each one of them and those who history books have not recorded. I'm grateful for their struggles, endurance, and strength that eradicated the notion that what we want to accomplish isn't possible. The beauty of you has destiny woven within and the will to do what seems to be impossible, possible. Here I put pen to paper and encourage those who are discouraged due to life circumstances to move forward with their dreams. You have the ingredients, be a success!

I Won't Be, is a declaration of freedom. It's about cutting loose! It shouts, find the value in you! It may be buried under years of disappointments, loss and hurt. This declaration can be a mandate for you. Anything less than you, just won't do. You are a person of mystery. Inside of you there lies a mind that can imagine wonders that no one else can imagine but you. Did you know that your imagination is a gift? Yes, God gave you this wonderful gift. I've read, "Nothing which you have imagined to do will be restrained from you."[17] Imagine your dreams and bring them to life. We all know what Walt Disney's imagination dreamt up, Mickey Mouse, Snow White and the Seven Dwarfs, Disney World, and all our favorite Disney movies.

You are an orchestrated frame by your Master Conductor. Like a beautiful, musical arrangement, He scored you on purpose. You are His heavenly accolade. You are a sleeping giant ready to be awakened by your desire for life. If the desire is not there, find out why. What voices have you been listening to that hinders you from becoming all that you can be? This is the resistance we talked about all through this book. This is the fight that you must win. I hope that I have laid out some strategies to help you win or at least see that you have a reason and the tools to launch your resistance. You can do more than you think, so think BIG, dream BIG!

RICHLY SCENTED

I LOVE CANDLES, ESPECIALLY THE ONES THAT ARE handmade with soy because of just that, they are handmade. I use those candles because they send an aroma throughout the house that lasts for days. When we give our all to be all that we can be, it's like we release the scent of our creativity. The best part of us is utilized when we open our desires and dreams for others to experience. When we use our creativity and abilities, we give back into this circle of life.

Our bad attitude about life can send out a bad odor of selfishness and self-absorbance. Remember, I said this isn't a selfish book. Instead, it encourages you to yield to life what life has placed in you no matter what that gift may be. It's like being a parent who fosters love and creativity in the young minds of their children be they a song writer, teacher, preacher, or artist. When we don't fight back to protect what's already ours, we cheat ourselves and those who would benefit from what we have inside of us. Outward beauty will fade but the scent of giving kindness, love, generosity and caring does a lot to a world that can sometimes seem hopeless.

The beauty of you is richly scented to make a positive difference to those around you. This book is also about making a difference, when you improve on yourself you give those around you the gift that is you. I love this last stanza because the thing that displays people's beauty is when they give of themselves at a cost. Facing challenge after challenge and continuing to move forward cost you something. Like the rose as it opens to greet the warmth of the light and releases its fragrance in the air, your beauty radiates and greets the world releasing a rich aroma to those all around you. Have you ever thought of yourself as beautiful?

You are richly scented to release love. The scent of love cannot be washed away. It's like the waters of the Great Lakes that flow to touch other parts of the world. It's nature and its beauty flows among the souls of people. In the Songs of Solomon, it describes a rose in the plains of Sharon in Palestine known as the rose of Sharon. This rose is said to be the most beautiful and perfect flower to bloom. It is richly scented and no other rose compares. This perfect rose has been compared to the sacrifice that Jesus Christ gave as the perfect gift and out of that perfect love, life was given to all mankind. He is the sweetest savor for the soul of man. "Oh, that men would praise the Lord for his goodness, and for his wonderful works to the children of men! For He satisfies the longing soul and fills the hungry soul with goodness" (King James Version, 1604, Ps. 107:8). During hardship, there is still far more beauty than you can see if you would just look in the mirror and see the beauty of you!

Tête-à-tête

Wow! Here you are. You made it through some tough moments. Even moments you felt you wouldn't finish this journey. Or maybe you stopped reading but picked this book back up again. Still, here we are together. I'm so proud of you. This book could have been your first step toward reaching your goals or maybe you're smack dab in the middle of many steps. You're still on your way to seeing your hard work pay off.

Thank you for taking time out of your precious life to read this book. Thank you for using ideas from this book to help you along the way. Most importantly, thank you for taking your life seriously enough to fight for it. Thanks for being courageous enough to remove any masks that have kept you in bondage to someone or something, even if you're the one holding them in place. However, you also have the power to take them off.

I hope you don't get tired of hearing me tell you that God loves you! If you don't have the faith to believe God loves you, then have enough courage to believe in you.

Although I haven't heard your voice or seen your face, I love you as well. I love you for making change where you saw necessary, seeking out help, and not being afraid of change. Maybe you were afraid but still rose to the challenge. Thank you for growing and being courageous. Thank you for giving me an opportunity to be a part of your journey. This is not the end so keep it moving. Your dreams are still ahead.

With much love,
Laurie

Final Exultation

Although you closed the pages to this book, I hope this book resonated within you and provided a positive experience. The declaration, "*I Won't Be*," is to get you motivated and push you onward. What else must you declare to make sure your dreams are realized? If you aren't living what you imagined, doing what you imagined or they're not tangible then you are not done. The point to this resistance is to win! If you need to go over some of the things we discussed, then do so. If you need to seek help on a professional level, then do it! Do whatever it takes to win. Remember the disclaimer? "This could become a messy resistance in which you take on full responsibility for the battle you must wage." You take responsibility to finish what you started. Don't give up!

One last thought don't allow your journal to be blank pages. Your heart is full of dreams and imageries that can make a positive difference in the world. Fill them with your ideas and dreams and make plans for them to come to life. Keep them always before your eyes. This last part is intentional as I know I've said it throughout this book, "Write the vision and make it plain on tablets, that he may run who reads it" (New King James Version, 1982, Hab. 2:2).

Declaration of You Questionnaire!

At the beginning of this book I mentioned, to declare who you are *not*, you must first know who you are.

Since the beginning of this journey, what have you discovered about yourself? Have you identified who you are?

What changes have you made since you first started reading? Are you the person you always thought you were?

Did any changes you make cause discomfort in relationships, work, or yourself?

What were your victories? What are the things you still need to work on?

If you haven't used a journal before, think about starting one because writing down the vision for your life will make a big impact on your success. Also, write down how you feel, your goals, dreams, and ideas to help you remember what you're striving for and how to obtain it.

Thank You!

Thank you so much for walking out this path with me. I hope this book made a positive impact on your life.

I have so much confidence in my declaration because Jesus is the Author and Finisher of my life. He is the reason I can confidently declare, "I won't be!" If your foundation isn't on Jesus, He's waiting to be your surety. You can have the same confidence and surety I have by confessing your need for Him to be your Lord and Savior.

Endnotes

1. Luke 21:19

2. September 1990 to December 1992 produced by Turner Program and DIC

3. differencebetween.com/difference-between-feelings-and-vs-emotions

4. Luke 6:45, Matthew 12:34

5. Blueletterbible.com

6. Wikipedia, dictionary.com, schoolhouse rock

7. eligious Beliefs and Psychiatry Posted Dec 10, 2010

8. Proverbs 4:10 Expanded Bible (EXB)

9. Habakkuk 2:2

10. Harvard University Chan Health https://www.hsph.harvard.edu/news/magazine/happiness-stress-heart-disease/

11. Psychology Today

[12] Bennett MP, Lengacher C. Humor and Laughter May Influence Health IV. Humor and Immune Function. Evid Based Complement Alternat Med. 2009;6(2):159-164.

[13] 2 Corinthians 4:7

[14] Psalms 16:8

[15] theroot.com/civil-rights-leaders-who-changed-history

[16] Speech before a group of students at Barratt Junior High School in Philadelphia, October 26, 1967

[17] Genesis 11:6

Printed in the USA
CPSIA information can be obtained
at www.ICGtesting.com
CBHW082138100224
4244CB00040B/742